FATHOM BIBLE STUDIES

FATH●M

A DEEP DIVE INTO THE STORY OF GOD

the bible

WHERE IT CAME FROM AND HOW TO READ IT

FATHOM: THE BIBLE
WHERE IT CAME FROM AND HOW TO READ IT
STUDENT JOURNAL

Writer: Bart Patton
Editor: Ben Howard
Designer: Keely Moore

Websites are constantly changing. Although the websites recommended in this resource were checked at the time this unit was developed, we recommend that you double-check all sites to verify that they are still live and that they are still suitable for students before doing the activity.

ISBN: 9781501837715

PACP10508408-01

17 18 19 20 21 22 23 24 25 26 — 10 9 8 7 6 5 4 3 2 1

MANUFACTURED IN THE UNITED STATES OF AMERICA

CONTENTS

About Fathom

Fathom.

It's such a big word. It feels endless and deep. It's the kind of word that feels like it should only be uttered by James Earl Jones with the bass turned all the way up.

Which means it's the perfect word to talk about a God who's infinite and awe-inspiring. It's also the perfect word for a book like the Bible that's filled with miracles and inspiration, but also wrestles with stories of violence and pain and loss.

The mission of *Fathom* is to dive deep into the story of God that we find in the Bible. You'll encounter Scriptures filled with inspiration and encouragement, and you'll also explore passages that are more complicated and challenging.

Each lesson will focus on one passage, but will also launch into the larger context of how God's story is being told through that passage. More importantly, each lesson will explore how God's story is intimately tied to our own stories, and how a God who is beyond our imagination can also be a God who loves us deeply and personally.

We invite you to wrestle with this and more as we dive deep into God's story.

Welcome

This book is yours. Or at least, it will be.

This book is designed to assist you as you explore, engage, and wrestle with everything that you'll experience over the next four weeks.

Each week during this study, this book will be filled with Scripture, activities, and questions to encourage and inspire you while you work your way through the Bible with your friends.

While we'll offer suggestions on how to use this journal, we want you to truly make it yours. Fill it with ideas and prayers. Take notes. Draw. Write poetry. Express yourself! Do whatever it is you need to do to help you remember what you've learned here.

Let this book be your canvas for creativity and self-expression. Let it be a place for honest questions and emotions that you may not feel comfortable expressing anywhere else, because at the end of this study, this book is yours.

You can use it to remember and reflect on what you learned, or you can use it to keep studying on your own, to keep questioning and exploring. We've included two sections at the end, "Takeaway" and "Explore More," to help you in that quest.

As you begin, we pray that you encounter the majesty and love of God through this study. We pray that you dive deep into the story of God and creation, and we pray that you find peace and hope in these lessons.

The Fathom 66

ENTER ZIP OR LOCATION [   ]

Stories ♡   [TICKETS]
★★★★★
Showtimes: Parts of Genesis, Joshua, Judges, Ruth, 1 Samuel,
2 Samuel, 1 Kings, 2 Kings, 1 Chronicles, 2 Chronicles, Ezra,
Nehemiah, Esther, Matthew, Mark, Luke, John, Acts

The Law ♡   [TICKETS]
★★★★★
Showtimes: Parts of Genesis, Exodus, Leviticus, Numbers,
Deuteronomy

Wisdom ♡   [TICKETS]
★★★★★
Showtimes: Job, Some Psalms, Proverbs, Ecclesiastes,
Song of Solomon, Lamentations, James

Psalms ♡   [TICKETS]
★★★★★
Showtimes: Psalms

The Prophets ♡   [TICKETS]
★★★★★
Showtimes: Isaiah, Jeremiah, Ezekiel, Hosea, Joel, Amos, Obadiah,
Jonah, Michah, Nahum, Habakkuk, Zephaniah, Haggai, Zechariah,
Malachi

Letters ♡   [TICKETS]
★★★★★
Showtimes: Romans, 1 Corinthians, 2 Corinthians, Galatians, Ephesians,
Philippians, Colossians, 1 Thessalonians, 2 Thessalonians, 1 Timothy, 2 Timothy,
Titus, Philemon, Hebrews, James, 1 Peter, 2 Peter, 1 John, 2 John, 3 John, Jude

Apocalyptic Writings ♡   [TICKETS]
★★★★★
Showtimes: Daniel, Revelation

The Fathom Bible Storylines

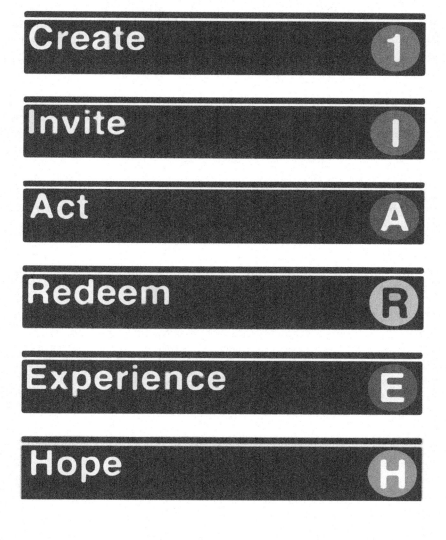

Create   1

Invite   I

Act   A

Redeem   ®

Experience   E

Hope   H

Introduction to The Bible

Background

The Bible we study today is a collection of 66 books—39 in the Old Testament and 27 in the New Testament—comprised of laws, histories, stories, poems, and letters exploring God's relationship with humanity. These books were originally written in three languages: Hebrew in the Old Testament, Greek in the New Testament, and Aramaic in the Books of Ezra and Daniel, as well as various other passages. Today the Bible is the most translated book of all time and is available in over five hundred different languages.

It only makes sense that a book written and compiled over hundreds of years by dozens of writers would be complicated and sometimes confusing. Add to that language differences and the need to wade through a variety of genres, and the Bible can look downright daunting.

This study is about empowering you to begin that task. Over the next four lessons, you'll learn about the history of the Bible and the types of stories it tells. More importantly, you'll learn and practice the methods you'll need to read and understand the Bible for yourself.

In some ways, the Bible is like a treasure chest. It's filled to the brim with riches, if only you can find the key to unlock it. It's a book filled with stories of courage and wisdom, inspiration and practical advice; but above all, it's a book that gives us insight into a God who is both far bigger than we can ever imagine and by our side at all times. This study, if you're willing, will help you find the key to unlocking this holy book and all that it has to offer.

Fathom Strategy for Reading and Understanding the Bible

"The Bible is written for us, but not to us."

This where we start on our quest. When we read the Bible, we have to constantly remember that the Bible is written for us, but not to us. Understanding the original context of the Bible helps us ask the right questions when interpreting Scripture.

For the first steps in our process, we need to understand how each passage we read functions in context and examine the historical background. When we read a passage, we should ask questions about the era, location, and culture of the original audience, as well as how a particular writing relates to the larger narrative of the Bible. This strategy not only helps us understand a passage's primary meaning, it also gives us guidance on how to translate that meaning into our specific circumstances today.

Working Definitions

Canon—the books of the Bible collectively recognized by the Christian church throughout time as inspired by God

Covenant—a solemn promise between God and God's people that defines their relationship to one another

Exegesis—the critical process of explaining and interpreting the Bible

Inductive Bible Study—a type of study that moves from generalized thoughts to specific application by using the Bible as the primary source of understanding

Lectio Divina (Divine Reading)—an ancient Latin practice of reading Scripture that involves reading, meditation, and prayer

A History of the Bible

Summary

I will gain an understanding of how we have come to have the Bible we read and use today.

Overview

- **Sync** with the concepts of transmission and translation through a group activity.
- **Tour** through the history of the Bible, exploring the key concepts of inspiration, transmission, and translation.
- **Reveal** how inspiration, transmission, and translation can affect our faith through journaling.
- **Build** understanding of the Christian tradition of translation through an activity allowing us to personalize the history we have learned.
- **After** the lesson, apply these ideas through activities that encourage the use of multiple translations of the Bible.

Anchor Point

- 2 Timothy 3:16-17—*Every Scripture is inspired by God and is useful for teaching, for showing mistakes, for correcting, and for training character, so that the person who belongs to God can be equipped to do everything that is good.*

SYNC   FATH●M

So You Think You Can Dance

Dance Teacher Instructions

This activity involved three processes: inspiration, transmission, and translation. The three dance teachers were inspired when they saw the original dance. Their writings transmitted the instructions of the dance. Then, your group translated the teacher's writings into a dance.

- 2 Timothy 3:16-17—*Every Scripture is inspired by God and is useful for teaching, for showing mistakes, for correcting, and for training character, so that the person who belongs to God can be equipped to do everything that is good.*

Inspiration—

Transmission—

Translation—

Translations of the Bible

Verbal Equivalence (Word for Word)	NASB
	KJV
	NKJV
	NRSV
	NIV
	CEB
Dynamic Equivalence (Thought for Thought)	NLT
Paraphrase	THE MESSAGE

History of the Bible Timeline

Pre-History	Oral traditions and storytelling
3200 BC	Early Mesopotamian/Sumerian writings
2000 BC	Birth of Abraham
2000–1500 BC	Book of Job written (possibly)
1500 BC	Moses receives the Law on Mount Sinai
1000 BC	Israel begins recording history; David is king
621 BC	Book of the Law discovered in temple by King Josiah (2 Kings 22)
587 BC	Jerusalem destroyed; ancient Israelite writings compiled in captivity
250–135 BC	Books of the Old Testament translated into Greek Septuagint
200 BC–AD 70	Dead Sea Scrolls transcribed in Essene community
AD 30	Ministry of Jesus
AD 52	Paul writes first letter to Thessalonian church
AD 70	Mark writes his Gospel
AD 80–90	Luke writes his Gospel and the Acts of the Apostles
AD 80–100	Matthew writes his Gospel
AD 100	Last of the New Testament books written
AD 350	Books and segments of the Bible translated into Latin
AD 383–405	Jerome translates the entire Bible into Latin, referred to as the Vulgate Bible
AD 393	Council of Hippo defines New Testament books
AD 397	Council of Carthage issues a complete canon of the Bible

AD 600–1100	Masoretic Text of Hebrew Scriptures compiled
AD 1225	Present system of chapters added
AD 1382	Bible translated into Middle English by John Wycliffe
AD 1455	Gutenberg makes first printed Bible with movable type (in Latin)
AD 1516	Erasmus publishes a Greek-Latin parallel New Testament
AD 1517	Luther starts the Protestant Reformation
AD 1526	Tyndale publishes the first English New Testament from Greek
AD 1539	The Great Bible published in English as the first authorized Bible of the Church of England
AD 1551	Present system of verses added
AD 1611	King James Version published in English
AD 1946–1956	981 Essene manuscripts found in caves near the Dead Sea (Old Testament)
AD 1978	New International Version published in English
AD 1989	New Revised Standard Version published in English
AD 2011	Common English Bible Version published in English

Journal Questions

1. How do you think differently about the Bible after today's lesson?

2. What is your personal understanding of inspiration?

3. What are some ways that you think other people understand inspiration, and how does that affect the way they treat the Bible?

4. Does God still speak to us through the Bible today? How?

BUILD

FATH●M

The Translators Late Show

Determine how your translator would have answered the two questions listed. Each team should select a representative to play the part of their translator in a talk-show-style interview format where they'll answer these questions.

The Questions:

1.   What inspired you to translate the Bible?

2.   Tell us what's special about your Bible translation.

Jerome

Jerome was a church elder and theologian—the protégé of Pope Damasus I—who lived in the fourth century. He is recognized by the Catholic Church as the patron saint of translators and librarians. As a young adult, he was a devoted scholar. While battling a grave illness in the year 374, he received a vision that caused him to surrender his life to God and the study of theology. After a stint with a monastic order in the Syrian desert, he came to be the secretary of the Pope. In Rome, he was assigned to translate the New Testament and Psalms into Latin from the Greek New Testament and Septuagint (a Greek translation of the Old Testament). The Church used this translation, called the Vulgate Bible, for centuries.

John Wycliffe

John Wycliffe was an English theologian, philosopher, and Oxford seminary professor during the fourteenth century. At the time, the Bible was only available in Latin, Greek, and Hebrew, and Wycliffe believed that the Bible should be translated into the common spoken language of the people. In this belief, he was at odds with the powerful Roman Catholic Church. He was disgusted by the corruption that he saw in church leadership, and believed that everyone should have the ability to read the Bible themselves, without it being interpreted for them by priests. In 1382, he and his followers, known as Lollards, completed a translation of the Latin Vulgate into Middle English. His translation was considered a rebellious act against the Church. This act, along with his sermons against excesses and abuses within the hierarchy of the Roman Catholic Church, led the Church to declare him a heretic at the Council of Constance in 1415, thirty-one years after his death. The Council also ordered all of his books and writings be burned. In 1428, Pope Martin V ordered that his body be exhumed and burned, and his ashes cast into a river. His work made the Bible accessible to laypeople and heavily influenced the early leaders of the Protestant Reformation.

King James

King James was raised in Scotland and was influenced by the early Presbyterian movement. When he took the throne of England in 1603 after Queen Elizabeth's death, there was a great division within the Church of England. Papists, Puritans, Presbyterians, and Separatists were all in disagreement over Christian traditions and matters of control within the state. Papists wanted England to return to the Roman Catholic Church. Puritans wanted to take the Reformation even further, eliminating all Catholic elements from the church. Presbyterians wanted to eliminate the hierarchy of church leadership. The Separatists wanted the state totally out of the church's affairs. Desperately desiring unity within the church, King James called together a conference to bring together leaders from all of the divided parties. Instead of addressing the petitions from the rival factions, James ordered a new, accurate, readable translation of the Bible, to be "read by the whole church." James believed a standard text could be unifying amidst a culture of discord. Before the King James Bible, different religious groups were further divided by their use of unique translations, commentaries, and prayer books. The King James Bible's authorization, as well as its beauty and scholarship, satisfied the demands of many diverse religious groups within England.

The Essenes

The Essenes were a small sect of religious Jews who held to a strict communal life. They were contemporaries of the Pharisees and Sadducees during the first century AD. They practiced voluntary poverty and daily washing rites for purification. They were devoted to charity as well as to communal prayer and meals. They did not believe in personal property and had strict laws concerning the sabbath. They often practiced celibacy. They were dedicated to a life of holiness and purity, and the study of the Scriptures was an important part of their daily life. The Essenes copied and preserved thousands of sacred Hebrew texts. Many of these were discovered in the mid-twentieth century in caves near the Dead Sea. These documents, known as the Dead Sea Scrolls, are some of the oldest surviving manuscripts of the biblical texts.

My Favorite Verse

Look up a favorite Bible verse on *www.biblegateway.com*. Select three different translations of the verse and note the differences and similarities. Finish by writing the verse in your own words.

An Encouraging Word

Find a Bible verse that would be an encouragement to a friend. Use *www.biblegateway.com* to choose the most appropriate translation. Text or direct-message this verse to your friend.

Inspiration Transmitted

Take a picture, or series of pictures, representing how you feel about God's faithfulness in the history of the Bible. Post it on social media with *#fathombible*. What image helps you to reflect on inspiration, transmission, and translation?

PRAYER FATH●M

God over all of time, we thank you for your great kindness and care in providing us with the Bible. Help us, in Jesus' name, to understand its life-changing message of love. Amen.

The Genres in the Bible

Summary

I will gain an understanding of the different genres in the Bible and how these genres affect the interpretation of Scripture.

Overview

- **Sync** the differences among genres through a group activity that focuses on interpreting the same message in different ways.
- **Tour** through an overview of the seven genres of biblical literature.
- **Reveal** awareness of the different genres in the Bible by writing a poem or song in the style of one of the seven Bible genres.
- **Build** understanding about the importance of recognizing different genres in the Bible through an interactive mapping exercise.
- **After** the lesson, contextualize understanding of the seven genres in the Bible with activities throughout the week.

Anchor Point

- 2 Timothy 2:15—*Make an effort to present yourself to God as a tried-and-true worker, who doesn't need to be ashamed but is one who interprets the message of truth correctly.*

Movie Madness Matchup

Comedy

Action

Horror

Western

Romance

Remaking Pinocchio

Group Treatment Genre:

Synopsis:

STORIES

Historical stories, genealogies, moral lessons, and parables.

The stories of the Bible are told through historical narratives, genealogies, and parables. When reading any story in the Bible, it is important to keep in mind these six characteristics of narrative: narrator, scene, characters, dialogue, plot, and structure.[1]

Examples: Genesis (parts), Joshua, Judges, Ruth, 1 Samuel, 2 Samuel, 1 Kings, 2 Kings, 1 Chronicles, 2 Chronicles, Ezra, Nehemiah, Esther, Matthew, Mark, Luke, John, Acts

Questions to Ask in Stories

The Narrator—*Who is telling the story?*
The Scene—*Where is the story taking place?*
The Characters—*Who is the story about?*
The Dialogue—*Who is talking, what are they saying, and who are they saying it to?*
The Plot—*What is the beginning, the middle, and the end of the story?*
The Structure—*How is the story told? Is it repeated anywhere else? Is it familiar?*

1. Gordon D. Fee and Douglas Stuart, *How to Read the Bible for All Its Worth: A Guide to Understanding the Bible* (Grand Rapids, MI: Zondervan, 1981), 93–98.

TOUR FATH●M

LAW

Legal documents and stories written to help God's people, Israel, understand their formation and relationship with God.

The books of the Law in the Old Testament—also known as the Torah, or Pentateuch—were written to help the people of Israel understand the rules of how they should live with one another as well as the rules of their relationship with God. This genre seeks to answer two questions: "How must we live as God's people in relationship to the Mosaic Covenant?" and "How must we live in God's presence?"

Examples: Genesis (parts), Exodus, Leviticus, Numbers, Deuteronomy

Questions to Ask in Law

How must we live as God's people in relationship to the Mosaic Covenant (the Law)?
How must we live in God's presence?

WISDOM

Life instructions based on observations and reflection meant to help people make godly choices.

Some verses in Wisdom literature can sound like lines from a fortune cookie. The Wisdom writings include life instructions focused on "applying God's truth to your life, so that your choices will indeed be godly."[2] They are poetic, observational, and comparative. They typically use simple verse patterns to compare and contrast axioms about the facts of life. They usually follow a pattern of four keys: listen, look, think, reflect.[3]

Examples: Job, some Psalms, Proverbs, Ecclesiastes, Song of Solomon, Lamentations, James

Keys to Observe in Wisdom

Listen!
Look!
Think!
Reflect!

2. Ibid., 225.
3. J. Scott Duvall and J. Daniel Hays, *Grasping God's Word: A Hands-On Approach to Reading, Interpreting, and Applying the Bible* (Grand Rapids, MI: Zondervan, 2001), 378.

TOUR FATH●M

PSALMS

The prayers and songs of God's people.

The Psalms are the prayers and songs of God's people. They help us learn how to express our emotions to God. We don't read songs the same way we do legal documents, letters, or stories. When reading a psalm, you should ask, "What is the emotion being expressed here?"

Example: Psalms

Question to Ask in Psalms

What emotion is being expressed?

THE PROPHETS

God speaks to Israel concerning the future of God's people because of their failure to obey the Law.

The prophetic books include the words of prophets called by God to spread a message concerning the future or a warning about the consequences of straying from God. The prophets spoke, wrote, and acted as the mouthpiece of God. The prophets used vivid and shocking imagery to illustrate Israel's rebellion and God's judgment. Social justice was a primary concern for the prophets as they emphasized Israel's failure to become the nation that God desired them to be.

Examples: Isaiah, Jeremiah, Ezekiel, Hosea, Joel, Amos, Obadiah, Jonah, Micah, Nahum, Habakkuk, Zephaniah, Haggai, Zechariah, Malachi

The Basic Message of the Prophets

1. You have broken the Mosaic Covenant; repent!
2. No repentance? Then judgment!
3. Yet, there is hope beyond judgment for a glorious restoration![4]

4. Ibid., 362.
FATHOM: The Bible

33

TOUR FATH●M

LETTERS

Written from church leaders to early congregations to address specific situations of doctrine, worship, and Christian living.

The New Testament consists largely of letters, sometimes called epistles. Early church leaders like Paul, Peter, and James wrote these letters to congregations across the Mediterranean world as the church expanded. While the letters address specific situations of doctrine, worship, and Christian living in those congregations, their messages are also deeply universal. The letters were read, copied, and passed around among the early churches, who were able to glean insights even though they were not the original audience. Today we continue to learn from these letters by following their example.

Examples: Romans, 1 Corinthians, 2 Corinthians, Galatians, Ephesians, Philippians, Colossians, 1 Thessalonians, 2 Thessalonians, 1 Timothy, 2 Timothy, Titus, Philemon, Hebrews, James, 1 Peter, 2 Peter, 1 John, 2 John, 3 John, Jude

Questions to Ask in Letters

Who is sending the message?
Who is receiving the message?
What's the reason (or reasons) for the communication?

APOCALYPTIC WRITINGS

Cryptic writings focused on future events that are based on divine revelation and visions.

Apocalyptic literature uses bold symbols and figurative language to discuss future events. Apocalyptic writings—whether understood literally or allegorically—serve to convey the hope of God's victory to those struggling to find meaning in difficult circumstances.

Examples: Daniel, Revelation

Question to Ask in Apocalyptic Writing

What are the symbols being used?
What do the symbols mean?

REVEAL FATH●M

My Psalm

BUILD

FATH●M

First Map Drawing:

Second Map Drawing:

Bible Genre Selfies

Take some time this week to take seven selfies—each one with a different expression that you believe represents a genre in the Bible. Have fun with this! Group them together or post them separately on social media with #fathombiblegenres.

Bible Genre Prayers

Take some time every day this week to write a two- or three-sentence short prayer. Create each one in the style of a different Bible genre. Write each one on a note card and make them your daily prayers.

Our Epistle

Working with other friends, write a short letter to your church in the way early church leaders like Paul wrote to local churches. With a positive tone, address concerns and areas that you feel need new consideration or attention. Encourage the church by spotlighting the ways you feel like it is doing well. Volunteer specific help and leadership that you would be willing to provide in order to facilitate new ideas. Return the letter to your youth leader and ask that it be read to church leaders.

PRAYER FATH●M

God of all wisdom, we praise you for your creativity in how you have expressed your story through the different genres of the Bible. Help us, in Jesus' name, to think well as we encounter each book contained within it. Amen.

The Storylines of the Bible

Summary

I will gain an understanding of the Bible's storylines and how they help us understand the story of God and creation.

Overview

- **Sync** the way we understand stories through a group activity.
- **Tour** through an overview of the central storylines in the Bible.
- **Reveal** the way these storylines continue in your life and help you understand our faith.
- **Build** understanding about how the meaning of a story shapes the way we tell it.
- **After** the lesson, look for these biblical storylines in your personal Bible study and every day in the world around us.

Anchor Point

- Deuteronomy 6:5-7—*Love the LORD your God with all your heart, all your being, and all your strength. These words that I am commanding you today must always be on your minds. Recite them to your children. Talk about them when you are sitting around your house and when you are out and about, when you are lying down and when you are getting up.*

Create

God is always creating and re-creating. We see this when God acts in the world in new and surprising ways.

The question we should ask about these passages is:

What new thing is God doing?

Examples: Genesis 1–3, Genesis 8, Joel 2:18-32, John 1, Romans 12, Revelation 21

Invite

God is constantly inviting humanity into a full and meaningful life, and a divine relationship. This is seen in the covenants that God makes with humanity throughout history.

The question we should ask about these passages is:

What is God's invitation?

Examples: Covenant with Noah (Genesis 9:7-11), Covenant with Abraham (Genesis 12:1-3), Covenant with Moses (Deuteronomy 11), Covenant with David (2 Samuel 7:8-16), New Covenant in Christ (Jeremiah 31:31-34; Hebrews 9:15)

Act

When God offers an invitation to humanity, God also gives humanity a choice in how they respond. We can see this in the way biblical figures decide to obey and accept or disobey and reject God's invitation. Many of the Bible's stories are about how individuals respond to God's reign and rule.

The question we should ask about these passages is:

How is this person or group choosing to respond to God's invitation?

Examples: Genesis 3, Genesis 6, Judges, 1 Kings, 2 Kings, Prophets, Acts

Redeem

God's work is about the redemption of all things. We see this redemption most clearly in the life and work of Jesus. Followers of Jesus are redeemed and join with the Holy Spirit to become agents of God's restorative work in the world.

The question we should ask about these passages is:

How is God working through this person, group, or situation to redeem, restore, and rebuild?

Examples: Psalm 18, Jonah 2, Gospels

Experience

God gives wisdom and direction for how to live a life empowered by the Holy Spirit. We see this in the writings of leaders who have left us a legacy of instruction from their encounters with God. This is where authentic faith meets real life in the quest for truth.

The question we should ask about these passages is:

How is the Holy Spirit leading and directing in these situations?

Examples: Job, Psalms, Proverbs, Ecclesiastes, New Testament Letters

Hope

God provides hope for the future. We see this often in prophetic writings by oppressed people in desperate situations. In the midst of what seem like impossible circumstances, God assures us of God's reign. Though things may not be right in the present, God promises a different outcome for those who endure.

The question we should ask about these passages is:

How is God assuring those in despair that they can have great faith in hope to come?

Examples: Daniel, Revelation

Genesis 4:9-16

The LORD said to Cain, "Where is your brother Abel?"
Cain said, "I don't know. Am I my brother's guardian?"
The LORD said, "What did you do? The voice of your brother's blood
is crying to me from the ground. You are now cursed from the ground
that opened its mouth to take your brother's blood from your hand.
When you farm the fertile land, it will no longer grow anything for you,
and you will become a roving nomad on the earth."
Cain said to the LORD, "My punishment is more than I can bear. Now
that you've driven me away from the fertile land and I am hidden from
your presence, I'm about to become a roving nomad on the earth, and
anyone who finds me will kill me."
The LORD said to him, "It won't happen; anyone who kills Cain will be
paid back seven times." The LORD put a sign on Cain so that no one
who found him would assault him. Cain left the LORD's presence, and he
settled down in the land of Nod, east of Eden.

Genre:

Storyline(s):

Psalm 13

How long will you forget me, LORD? Forever?
   How long will you hide your face from me?
How long will I be left to my own wits,
   agony filling my heart? Daily?
How long will my enemy keep defeating me?

Look at me!
   Answer me, LORD my God!
Restore sight to my eyes!
   Otherwise, I'll sleep the sleep of death,
      and my enemy will say, "I won!"
   My foes will rejoice over my downfall.

But I have trusted in your faithful love.
   My heart will rejoice in your salvation.
Yes, I will sing to the LORD
   because he has been good to me.

Genre:

Storyline(s):

Jeremiah 31:31-34

The time is coming, declares the Lᴏʀᴅ, when I will make a new covenant with the people of Israel and Judah. It won't be like the covenant I made with their ancestors when I took them by the hand to lead them out of the land of Egypt. They broke that covenant with me even though I was their husband, declares the Lᴏʀᴅ. No, this is the covenant that I will make with the people of Israel after that time, declares the Lᴏʀᴅ. I will put my Instructions within them and engrave them on their hearts. I will be their God, and they will be my people. They will no longer need to teach each other to say, "Know the Lᴏʀᴅ!" because they will all know me, from the least of them to the greatest, declares the Lᴏʀᴅ; for I will forgive their wrongdoing and never again remember their sins.

Genre:

Storyline(s):

John 3:1-8

There was a Pharisee named Nicodemus, a Jewish leader. He came to Jesus at night and said to him, "Rabbi, we know that you are a teacher who has come from God, for no one could do these miraculous signs that you do unless God is with him."

Jesus answered, "I assure you, unless someone is born anew, it's not possible to see God's kingdom."

Nicodemus asked, "How is it possible for an adult to be born? It's impossible to enter the mother's womb for a second time and be born, isn't it?"

Jesus answered, "I assure you, unless someone is born of water and the Spirit, it's not possible to enter God's kingdom. Whatever is born of the flesh is flesh, and whatever is born of the Spirit is spirit. Don't be surprised that I said to you, 'You must be born anew.' God's Spirit blows wherever it wishes. You hear its sound, but you don't know where it comes from or where it is going. It's the same with everyone who is born of the Spirit."

Genre:

Storyline(s):

Romans 5:6-11

While we were still weak, at the right moment, Christ died for ungodly people. It isn't often that someone will die for a righteous person, though maybe someone might dare to die for a good person. But God shows his love for us, because while we were still sinners Christ died for us. So, now that we have been made righteous by his blood, we can be even more certain that we will be saved from God's wrath through him. If we were reconciled to God through the death of his Son while we were still enemies, now that we have been reconciled, how much more certain is it that we will be saved by his life? And not only that: we even take pride in God through our Lord Jesus Christ, the one through whom we now have a restored relationship with God.

Genre:

Storyline(s):

Revelation 16:1-7

Then I heard a loud voice from the temple say to the seven angels, "Go and pour out the seven bowls of God's anger on the earth." So the first angel poured his bowl on the earth, and a nasty and terrible sore appeared on the people who had the beast's mark and worshipped its image. The second angel poured his bowl into the sea, and the sea turned into blood, like the blood of a corpse, and every living thing in the sea died. The third angel poured his bowl into the rivers and springs of water, and they turned into blood. Then I heard the angel of the waters say,

"You are just, holy one, who is and was,
    because you have given these judgments.
They poured out the blood of saints and prophets,
    and you have given them blood to drink. They deserve it!"
And I heard the altar say,
    "Yes, Lord God Almighty, your judgments are true and just."

Genre:

Storyline(s):

REVEAL FATH●M

Journal Questions

1. How does understanding these storylines help you understand God's relationship with creation?

2. How do you see these storylines playing out in your own faith?

3. Which storyline connects with you most strongly? Why?

New Story, Same As the Old?

AFTER FATH●M

I Walk the Storyline

During your personal Bible study time this week, make notes of where you see the six storylines in the Bible: create, invite, act, redeem, experience, and hope. While reading and reflecting on the verses, ask yourself which of the storylines you see at work. Keep these notes and reminders in the margin of your Bible or a journal. If you are reading through a chapter or book of the Bible, track the progression and overlap of the storylines. Use colored pencils or highlighters to mark storylines.

#FathomStoryline

The great thing about the storylines we see in the Bible is that they are still playing out as part of God's story today. Take some pictures this week of things in your world in which you see the six storylines of the Bible at work: create, invite, act, redeem, experience, and hope. Post the pictures on social media with *#fathomstoryline*, and comment on which storyline you see.

Living Out the Lines

Spend some time this week reflecting on how God has worked in your life's story. Journal about how you see God actively writing an incredible saga through your journey. Identify and explore all six storylines in the past and present. Ask a friend to do the same and share your reflections with each other.

PRAYER FATH●M

God of every moment, we glorify you for your care as you have crafted every moment of history to tell us your story. Help us, in Jesus' name, to truly fathom the constructs of that story—and to find our own storylines within them—as we study the Bible. Amen.

How to Interpret the Bible

Summary

I will learn and practice how to read and study the Bible using the Fathom Exegetical Process.

Overview

- **Sync** the importance of the concepts of light and context when reading the Bible.
- **Tour** through the Fathom Exegetical Process.
- **Reveal** how the Bible can be applied to our lives using *Lectio Divina* as part of the Fathom Exegetical Process.
- **Build** confidence in using the Fathom Exegetical Process by using the process on a favorite hymn or praise song.
- **After** the lesson, practice using the Fathom Exegetical Process at home.

Anchor Point

- Psalm 119:105—*Your word is a lamp before my feet and a light for my journey.*

Loopy Locution

The Words

1. Job Title (Noun)   _____

2. Thing (Noun)   _____

3. Verb (Present Tense)   _____

4. Adjective   _____

5. Adjective   _____

6. Place (Noun)   _____

7. Living Thing (Noun)   _____

8. Verb (Present Tense)   _____

9. Adjective   _____

10. Adjective   _____

11. Noun   _____

12. Verb (Present Tense)   _____

13. Place (Noun)   _____

14. Noun   _____

SYNC FATH●M

15.   Two Celebrities   _____

                                   _____

16.   Noun   _____

17.   Noun   _____

18.   Person in the Room   _____

19.   Verb (Present Tense)   _____

20.   Piece of Furniture (Noun) _____

21.   Verb (Present Tense)   _____

22.   Recipe Ingredient (Noun)   _____

23.   Noun   _____

24.   Noun   _____

25.   Adjective   _____

26.   Verb (Present Tense)   _____

27.   Person in the Room (Possessive) _____

28.   Verb (Present Tense)   _____

29.   Structure (Noun)   _____

30.   Verb (Present Tense)   _____

The Passage

The LORD is my (1) _____.

I lack (2) _____.

He lets me (3) _____ in

(4) _____ meadows;

he leads me to (5) _____ (6) _____ ;

he keeps (7) _____ alive.

He (8) _____ me in (9) _____ paths

for the sake of his (10) _____ (11) _____ .

Even when I (12) _____ through the

darkest (13) _____ ,

I fear no (14) _____

because (15) _____ [and] _____

are with me.

Your (16) _____ and your (17) _____ —

they protect (18) _____ .

SYNC

FATH●M

You (19) _____ a (20) _____

    for me right in front of my enemies.

You (21) _____ my head in (22) _____ ;

    my (23) _____ is so full it spills over!

Yes, (24) _____ and (25) _____ love

    will (26) _____ me all the days of

    (27) _____ life,

    and I will (28) _____ in the LORD's

    (29) _____

    as long as I (30) _____ .

TOUR FATH●M

Psalm 119:105—*Your word is a lamp before my feet and a light for my journey.*

Fathom Strategy for Reading and Understanding the Bible

The Bible is written for us, not to us.

The Fathom Exegetical Process

Floodlight (The Big Picture)—Floodlights illuminate large areas with wide, dispersed lighting. A floodlight shows the whole picture. Connect the verse or passage to its place in the whole of the biblical narrative.

Questions to ask: *Where does the passage fall in the big story of the Bible? Which storyline is it emphasizing?*

Flashlight (The Focused Context)—Flashlights illuminate smaller areas with directed, focused lighting. A flashlight shows a specific focal target. Connect the verse or passage to its immediate context.

Questions to ask: *What is the genre of the passage? Who was the original intended audience? What was its purpose to the original audience? What did it mean to them?*

Headlight (In Front of Us)—Car headlights illuminate the road ahead of a moving vehicle with reflected, projected lighting. A headlight shows a progressing, dynamic pathway. Connect the verse or passage to our own day.

Questions to ask: *What could the passage be saying about God or God's reign today? What does this mean now to the church on the other side of the cross? How does this speak right now?*

Shadow (A Glimpse of Jesus)—A shadow is produced when an object comes between a surface and a source of light. A shadow does not reflect or show light, but is evidence of the light. Connect the verses to the person and work of Jesus. The text might not speak at all about Jesus, but we can still learn something about his character, ministry, and context—even if it's simply humanity's great need for the redemption he provides.

Question to ask: *How does this passage help me understand the person and work of Jesus?*

Laser (Personal Application)—Lasers illuminate tiny areas with powerful, focused light. Laser light is strong enough to cut through material objects and surfaces. Connect the passage with a personal application for you, the reader. It is helpful to practice *Lectio Divina* before arriving at a personal application. In *Lectio Divina*, the reader simply reads the passage with a clear mind, meditates in silence, and prays—listening for God's voice. Pay close attention to the words or phrases that stand out from your Bible reading.

Questions to ask: *What does the passage mean for me? How then shall I live?*

TOUR   FATH●M

Navigating the Method

1 John 1:5-7

This is the message that we have heard from him and announce to you: "God is light and there is no darkness in him at all." If we claim, "We have fellowship with him," and live in the darkness, we are lying and do not act truthfully. But if we live in the light in the same way as he is in the light, we have fellowship with each other, and the blood of Jesus, his Son, cleanses us from every sin.

Acts 1:8

Rather, you will receive power when the Holy Spirit has come upon you, and you will be my witnesses in Jerusalem, in all Judea and Samaria, and to the end of the earth.

Floodlight (The Big Picture)

Where does the passage fall in the big story of the Bible? Which storyline is it emphasizing?

Storyline(s):

How does this passage fit into the big story of the Bible?

Flashlight (The Focused Context)

What is the genre of the passage? Who was the original intended audience? What was its purpose to the original audience?

Biblical Genre:

What is the original context of this passage?

TOUR   FATH●M

Headlight (In Front of Us)

What could the passage be saying about God or God's reign today? How does this speak right now?

What are the differences between the original context and audience and today's context and audience?

What does this passage mean today?

Shadow (A Glimpse of Jesus)

How does this passage help me understand the person and work of Jesus?

64

REVEAL FATH●M

Navigating the Method

Laser (Personal Application)

What does the passage mean for me? How then shall I live?

Practice *Lectio Divina*. (Read, meditate, and pray in silence.)

What words or phrases stand out?

What is the passage saying to you today? (Be specific.)

BUILD FATH●M

Shine a Light

Song:

Floodlight:

Flashlight:

Headlight:

Shadow:

Laser:

AFTER FATH●M

Rays-of-Light Photo Challenge

Capture an interesting picture of each example of light from the Fathom Exegetical Process (floodlight, flashlight, headlight, shadow, laser). Be as creative as you want! Post them to social media using *#fathombiblelights*, with comments about how you are seeing God's story in new ways through personal Bible study.

Using the Fathom Exegetical Process

Select a Bible passage from the list below and use the Fathom Exegetical Process to arrive at your personal application this week. Commit to sharing the highlights of your study with a small-group leader, youth leader, pastor, parent, or friend.

Jeremiah 29:8-14
Acts 8:26-40
Philippians 4:10-14

Choose to Act

With other friends from your group, find a way to serve in your local community this week. Allow this to be a response to God's invitation. Ask your youth leader to help you find some different opportunities to serve—food pantries, roadside cleanups, nursing homes, hospitals, homeless missions, military/veteran support, and so forth.

PRAYER FATH●M

God of wisdom, we humbly accept the gift you have given us in the Bible. Help us, in Jesus' name, to delight in its words as we find strength, hope, wisdom, and help in our lifelong study of them. Amen.

Takeaway

I met John years ago at a small church in New York. He would always sit in the front pew with his young family on Sundays. When I would preach, he was locked in on every word and took copious notes. When it came time to explain the Scriptures in the sermon, I could see the wheels begin to turn and his eyes would light up as his head bobbed in enthusiastic discovery. He was always the first in line after the service to say something encouraging about my sermon and the Scriptures I'd used. John would tell me exactly how he intended to live out the lesson he had received. He was clearly hungry for the Bible in his life.

After several months, I invited him to get involved in a small-group Bible study. He always kindly, but sadly, refused the offer. Finally, after multiple rejections, I asked why. "I'm scared to study the Bible," he responded. "When I was young, I watched others use the Bible to hurt people—as a defense to keep away people they didn't like or agree with. I'm afraid that if I really start to study the Bible, one day it's going to tell me to be like that."

John wasn't afraid of submitting his life to the instructions found in the Bible; instead, he feared becoming arrogant and using the knowledge he'd found to hurt others. John was desperate for the truth found in Scripture, but he saw the Bible as something so loaded, so complicated and confusing that he was afraid of the very book that he was so passionate about on Sunday mornings. No doubt, you have seen the Bible misused like John had. Like him, it may have even caused you to keep a healthy distance from it and those who invite its serious study.

This study has equipped you with a basic knowledge of the Bible's history and structure. Through these four lessons, you now have a solid understanding of the literary and historical context of the Bible, and a reliable method for personal study.

This newfound knowledge means you're faced with a choice. You can choose to use this knowledge to move you beyond the kind of fear John had into a healthy, working relationship with the Bible or you can choose to put away these tools. If you choose the first path, I promise it will be challenging to you. You'll encounter things in your life that you need to change, and you'll see the world through a new lens. It is likely that you will never be the same.

If you choose the second path, and many do, it will probably be easier, but you will miss out on the fruit of working with the Bible and the thrill of personal transformation as you work toward who God created you to be.

I pray that God would drive away fear, confusion, apathy, and rigidity from your hearts when it comes to the Bible. May this study be about far more than facts, methodology, history, education, and doctrine. May you encounter the Bible as God has intended and find yourselves deeply rooted in the love of God through the living words of the Holy Bible.

Explore More

James 1:22-25

You must be doers of the word and not only hearers who mislead themselves. Those who hear but don't do the word are like those who look at their faces in a mirror. They look at themselves, walk away, and immediately forget what they were like. But there are those who study the perfect law, the law of freedom, and continue to do it. They don't listen and then forget, but they put it into practice in their lives.

Application

• The balance of knowledge and action is crucial to transformational Bible study. The goal is to stay balanced and move ahead. We must allow our knowledge of the Bible to transform our daily living.

Questions

1. How often do you look in the mirror? How does this metaphor help us to think about the Bible?
2. What are some ways that you can ensure a balance between knowledge and action in your personal Bible study?

Psalm 1:1-3

The truly happy person
doesn't follow wicked advice,
doesn't stand on the road of sinners,
and doesn't sit with the disrespectful.
Instead of doing those things,
these persons love the LORD's Instruction,
and they recite God's Instruction day and night!
They are like a tree replanted by streams of water,
which bears fruit at just the right time
and whose leaves don't fade.
Whatever they do succeeds.

Application

• Psalm 1 is a "wisdom psalm." Long ago, it was selected to be the introduction to the Book of Psalms for its comprehensive message about the importance of applying the words of the Lord to our daily lives.

Questions

1. What do you think it means to "love the LORD's Instruction"?
2. How do you believe that devotion, passion, and commitment to Scripture can produce godly fruit in your life?

CPSIA information can be obtained
at www.ICGtesting.com
Printed in the USA
LVOW13s0812110417
530325LV00002BA/5/P